Living in Peace

Companion in Faith

Living in Peace

Fr. Jeffrey Kirby, STD

Our Sunday Visitor
Huntington, Indiana

Nihil Obstat
Msgr. Michael Heintz, Ph.D.
Censor Librorum

Imprimatur
✠ Kevin C. Rhoades
Bishop of Fort Wayne-South Bend
August 21, 2020

The *Nihil Obstat* and *Imprimatur* are official declarations that a book is free from doctrinal or moral error. It is not implied that those who have granted the *Nihil Obstat* and *Imprimatur* agree with the contents, opinions, or statements expressed.

Except where noted, the Scripture citations used in this work are from the *Revised Standard Version of the Bible — Second Catholic Edition* (Ignatius Edition), copyright © 1965, 1966, 2006 National Council of the Churches of Christ in the United States of America. Used by permission. All rights reserved.

Every reasonable effort has been made to determine copyright holders of excerpted materials and to secure permissions as needed. If any copyrighted materials have been inadvertently used in this work without proper credit being given in one form or another, please notify Our Sunday Visitor in writing so that future printings of this work may be corrected accordingly.

Our Sunday Visitor Publishing Division, Our Sunday Visitor, Inc., 200 Noll Plaza, Huntington, IN 46750; www.osv.com; 1-800-348-2440.

ISBN: 978-1-68192-758-9 (Inventory No. T2627)
RELIGION—Christian Living—Inspirational
RELIGION—Christian Living—Spiritual Growth
RELIGION—Christianity—Catholic

eISBN: 978-1-68192-759-6
LCCN: 2020944547

Cover design: Tyler Ottinger
Cover art: Adobe Stock
Interior design: Chelsea Alt

PRINTED IN THE UNITED STATES OF AMERICA

CONTENTS

Introduction

In the spring of 2020, the world was struck by a global pandemic. Every nation responded differently. The United States chose to enter into a national quarantine in order to prevent the spread of the virus.

People were confused, scared, and frustrated. Many lost their jobs or were furloughed. The market bounced, and necessary cleaning resources ran out. Families were restricted to their homes, and we saw a rise in marital tension and domestic violence. Schools suspended on-site teaching, and students had to receive digital instruction. Parks were closed, and many of our entertainment and leisure outlets went on hiatus. Churches also closed their doors, and Catholics endured the suspension of public Masses for many weeks.

It was a time of widespread uncertainty and restlessness.

During the quarantine, Christian believers celebrated Easter, the solemnity of the Lord's resurrection. Unable to attend Easter services in person, many of the faithful streamed them online, praying in the midst of confusion, uncertainty, and a sense of abandonment. During the fifty-day Easter season that followed, the series of reflections contained in this book were first given to believers as a source of hope and a call to mission.

While they were initially meant to serve as encouragement in the face of the COVID-19 pandemic, these reflections are not limited to a time of quarantine. With their focus on striving after peace so we can live our Christian call, they remain relevant for any time and any season of life, especially when we face moments of stress and anxiety. These reflections are meant as a source of consolation, a help toward clarity of mind and heart, and as a summons to fulfill our commission to be instruments of the Risen Christ, working to share his peace with our world today.

As you read and pray upon these reflections, which were born from the trenches of real life and given in a time of great need, I pray you will be blessed with peace and hope. And as you receive these spiritual gifts, I ask you to graciously share them with others. Additionally, please consider passing along a copy of these reflections to your friends, family members, and other loved ones.

May the God of all peace bless you. May the God of hope visit you and lift you up!

.. I ..

THE PEACE OF GOD

Jesus came and stood among them and said to them, "Peace be with you."

John 20:19

Life is good. Life is beautiful. Life is a blessing. But sometimes it doesn't feel that way. Days get long. Responsibilities and expectations increase. Time flies. We feel like we have a hundred different things that are pulling us in a hundred different directions. In such situations, we acutely feel our limitations. Stress abounds.

Life's responsibilities don't end with our tiredness. Bills don't stop coming because we don't like them — or even when we can't afford them. Tension in families and other relationships doesn't wait for it to be a good or convenient time. When life presents us with challenges, kindness and charity seem like distant fantasies. In response to such heaviness, we can speak rashly and get defensive too quickly. Anxiety appears to be the rule of the day. Life can just seem to be one big burden.

But there is good news! Though they can seem never-ending, the duties, responsibilities, heaviness, and tensions of our lives also have limitations. They do not have to define who we are or how we live. They might compete for our souls; they might rally to overrun us and empty our hearts of their richness. Their attacks might leave us spiritually scarred, but they do not have to overwhelm us.

The Lord Jesus comes and says to us, as he did to the apostles when they were confused and scared in the Upper Room, "Peace be with you." With this bold, life-giving declaration, he exposes the chaos of our lives, names our burdens, and offers us a new and invigorating power that allows us to reclaim the beauty and redirect the narrative of our lives.

In the Risen Christ's earth-shaking pronouncement of peace, we receive an overflowing affirmation of our true identity as the children of God. We are not the children of chaos or of frenzy. We are not the children of stress. We are the children of God, and peace is our inheritance!

In the peace that comes with the Lord's resurrection, the darkness of our world has been scattered. We have been unyoked from the world's heaviness and freed from slavery to its hustle and bustle. The heaviness of this world has been deflated. It only has the power we give it. Yes, the darkness is still on the periphery, and it periodically whispers to us. But in the Resurrection, we have peace and an authority from on high to name the darkness and exorcise it.

We are the children of God! We are the children of peace. We are the children of glory.

In the Resurrection, we receive eyes of faith, and this faith gives us an infinite horizon. We are able to see God's presence in the ups and downs of our lives. We can see all the tasks and duties, sorrows and joys of this world in the light of eternity. In this perspective, the difficulties and sufferings of this life become smaller and more manageable. This new perspective can invigorate us to greater heights and more noble aspirations.

This is not a dream, removed idealism, escapism, or wishful thinking. The peace of God, which is beyond all understanding, is more real and tangible than anything else in this world. The peace of God empowers us to enter the trenches of life with the sure knowledge that we are loved, and that we have the strength to carry and conquer whatever is given to us and whatever is permitted to befall us.

As the Lord declares peace, he shows us his pierced hands and side. He reveals to us the sufferings of his Passion. He invites us — with Saint Thomas — to probe his wounds and touch his side. He offers us this intimacy as a sign of his love and as a proof of his sincerity. He shows us that he too has suffered. He humbles himself and unveils to us the wounds of this life.

The Lord is no idealist. He announces peace to us, even as he shows us the effects of this world's darkness upon himself. The Lord's wounds are his credibility. They shout out the legitimacy of his message of peace. Only a person who has endured such evils could convincingly speak about the peace of God. Only a person who has carried the heaviness — and suffered from the burdens — of this life could be taken seriously as he announces peace from on high. Only a person who has been in the darkness and has overcome it is competent to speak of peace. Only such a person is worthy of our trust.

By the wounds of the Lord Jesus, therefore, we are led out of the darkness of this world. By his wounds we are healed. By his wounds and the glory of his resurrection we are given the peace of God.

We do not have to be weighed down under the passing things of this world. We do not have to submit to desolation, self-pity, negativity, bitterness, or resentment.

As the Christian tradition has always sung, we are an Easter people and "Alleluia" is our song. We have been blessed with the gift of peace. And now we are to redirect our energy and redouble our efforts to receive God's peace and then become instruments of that peace to others.

WISDOM FOR OUR LIVES
In difficult times, when we feel overwhelmed by the heaviness of life, let us look to the Lord Jesus. Allow him to show us his wounds and say to us, "Peace be with you." Accept that peace. Share that peace with others.

PRAYER
Heavenly Father,
There are so many things that demand our
    attention,
so many duties that must be fulfilled,
so much stress and anxiety that threaten to
    overtake our souls.
Help us!
Lord Jesus,
You are the Beginning and End of all things.
Come to us.
Calm the storms of this life.
Heal us by your wounds.
Proclaim your peace in our lives.
Give us this peace.
Show us the Father.
Point us to eternal things.

Save us!
For you are Lord, forever and ever.
Amen.

·· II ··

THE CALL OF MERCY

*When he had said this, he breathed on them,
and said to them, "Receive the Holy Spirit. If you
forgive the sins of any, they are forgiven; if you
retain the sins of any, they are retained."*
John 20:22–23

Few needs in this life — whether real or perceived — can compete with the compelling need that we have in our innermost being to both receive and give mercy.

In order to humble ourselves and say, "I was wrong" or "I was hurtful" or "I purposely harmed you or betrayed you," we need a profound sense of humility. At the same time, it takes an extreme level of compassion to hear these words from another and to offer mercy. It takes even more compassion to offer mercy without hearing these words.

Such humility and compassion require a strength that is beyond us. We need help to come to this level of self-accusation and to this degree of kindness. The Lord knows that we need this help, and he comes to our aid.

The risen Lord proclaims his peace to us. In that same moment, he gives us the Holy Spirit and calls us to forgive others and to receive forgiveness. Thus the singular distinctive mark of the Christian is our desire for peace, expressed by our willingness to ask for mercy and to generously give it to others.

The Christian message of mercy is a divine gift. As such, it has always been viewed as a radical message in our fallen world. It rocked the ancient world when Christians first began to say, "I forgive you." It shakes up our world today. Our wayward minds and hearts struggle to understand the dismissal of vengeance and the bestowal of mercy.

But where does the power come from to forgive and to ask for forgiveness? Yes, certainly, we receive it by the power of the Holy Spirit. But the Holy Spirit doesn't work in a vacuum. Oftentimes the Spirit will work through other people. He brought about the Incarnation of the Son of God through a virgin in Nazareth. He shepherds the universal Church through a bishop in Rome, who is a sinner like the rest of us. The Holy Spirit also works through other means, including creation — he brings the presence of the Lord Jesus to us under the appearance of bread and wine at Mass.

So how does the Holy Spirit move us to seek and receive mercy?

In the Upper Room, the Jesus breathed on the apostles. He breathed on them! It's both an affectionate and Spirit-filled action. And when he breathed on them, he breathed on *them* — that is, all of them. He did not breathe on any apostle alone. He breathed on them as a community. The apostles and Our Lady received the Holy Spirit as a community. Jesus gave the commission to give and to receive mercy, therefore, not to one person alone, but within a community of faith.

This simple reality shows us how the Holy Spirit will accomplish our summons to mercy.

After the apostolic community received the Holy Spirit, they began to imitate and live according to the way they saw the Lord live. They began to follow "the way." It is not a coincidence that the early members of the Church were simply called "members of the way." Only later did we receive the name "Christian" from those who witnessed the way of life of the early disciples.

Throughout the Acts of the Apostles we see the marks of the Christian way of life. In the sacred narrative we can discern what it means to be a Christian community. This community is essential since it is the laboratory — the proving grounds and springboard — for us to live a life of mercy.

In the Acts of the Apostles we see that the Christian community is one that celebrates the sacraments, especially the Eucharist (the "breaking of the bread" [Acts 2:42]). They also pray together, share holy fellowship, study the apostolic teachings, and selflessly serve the poor and those in need.

These are the signs of a community consecrated to the Lord Jesus and committed to a ministry of mercy. If we are to fulfill our call to mercy, we also must share an active community life together. Christians need one another. When we are together, the Lord is with us. We are made strong and find the inner fortitude to die to ourselves, to live abundantly in Christ, and to humbly seek and generously give mercy.

We need holy fellowship. It is no mistake that of the thirteen apostolic letters written by Saint Paul, the one thing he most emphasizes is the utter importance of the Christian to be with other Christians. He emphasizes the great need for holy fellowship. We cannot have peace by living this life alone. Holy fellowship helps us to forgive those who have hurt us, or those who have harmed our loved ones. We need one another if we are going to live a life of peace and faithfully carry out our call to mercy. We need one another's encouragement, affirmation, and exhortation. We need the help of other believers to carry our cross and to be a worthy instrument of mercy in our world today.

We are Christians, sons and daughters of the Resurrection, united by the Holy Spirit, and we should exercise that power. We are called to use it, to put it to work!

There is no room in our community for bitterness, vengeance, self-pity, or rage. We were not created for a life of constant tension. We were created for glory. We are offered true peace in Jesus Christ. We are called to be recipients of mercy and to be instruments of peace to those around us.

Today, the Lord Jesus breathes on us. Let us be inspired by this act of affection and nurture our Christian communities. The more we follow the way of the Lord, the more the Holy Spirit will be able to work through us, and the more softened and inclined our hearts will be to ask for mercy and to give it to others. This enables us to live the life of peace that Jesus won for us by his saving death and resurrection.

Wisdom for Our Lives

As we struggle to ask for mercy, or to give mercy to those who need it, the Lord Jesus breathes on us. Let us receive his Spirit. Let us confidently turn to our fellow believers for strength and encouragement.

PRAYER
Heavenly Father,
There is so much suffering and hurt in our
     world.
We are a fallen race and a sinful people.
Give us your blessing!
Lord Jesus,
you are the Divine Mercy and the Healer of
     Souls.
Open our hearts.
Forgive us our offenses.
Strengthen us to forgive others.
Help us to live up to your call of mercy.
Guide us.
Show us the Father.
Point us to everlasting peace.
Save us!
For you are Lord, forever and ever.
Amen.

·· III ··

THE STRENGTH OF GOD

That very day two of them were going to a village named Emmaus, about seven miles from Jerusalem, and talking with each other about all these things that had happened. While they were talking and discussing together, Jesus himself drew near and went with them.

Luke 24:13–15

The Christian faith is not a religion for wimps. And it doesn't make us wimpy, either. Instead, it calls us to denounce the evil spirits of indulgence, rash anger, entitlement, and self-pity, and to live in a spirit of freedom, love, and hope.

The Christian faith is a strong way of life. There's power in following the Lord Jesus. We see it in his passion and death, when he conquered all the fallen spirits of our world. The

Lord destroyed the kingdom of sin and death, and he gives us his grace to make us strong and continue his fight. He sealed the deal with his glorious resurrection.

We are the children of the Resurrection. We are the sons and daughters of God. We have received his grace, which is his own life and power within us. Grace makes us strong. There's no room in our hearts for wimpy or fallen spirits.

But we know that we are fallen. At times we address our struggles by sleeping in, staying up to ungodly hours, binging on television shows, or getting impatient and abrupt with family members. We become negligent in our work, and we may even begin to hide from pain with pornography, prescription drugs, alcohol, or other addictions. It appears at times that the battle of life just gets the best of us. But our faith is not a religion for wimps!

We worship a God who carried a cross, endured a passion, and suffered crucifixion — and who rose in glory! And the same Spirit that raised the Lord Jesus from the dead dwells in each of us. And so, in Christ, we are made strong. We are given his grace to persevere, to keep holding on, to endure this battle, and to be victorious.

The sufferings of this life will pass. They are incomparable to the grace of God and the majesty of his glory, which he offers to each of us. Despite how we might feel, we must dig deep and hold on to what we know. In the Risen Christ, we will get through the difficulties that are a part of our fallen world. The heaviness and hardships of our lives are not the end, and they do not define us. They do not define our faith. They do not define our state of affairs. Try as they might, they do not define our world. The sorrows and sufferings of the world have no power over us. We will walk through this valley of the shadow of darkness, knowing that our Good Shepherd — the Risen Christ, the strong and powerful Lord — is guiding us and giving us his strength.

This is not a religion for wimps. There is no room for compromise, false accommodation, overindulgence, or self-pity. In the name of the Risen Christ, we send these dark spirits back to hell where they belong. They do not belong in the heart of a person consecrated to Jesus Christ.

The account of the two disciples on the way to Emmaus helps us to understand the gift of peace given to us by the Risen Christ. We can see how he turns confused, scared, and distracted hearts into peaceful hearts; how he turns wimpy hearts into strong hearts that burn with hope and a sense of mission.

The two disciples had given up. We are told they were leaving the holy city Jerusalem. They wanted to leave behind the place where Jesus died, but, in reality, they were leaving the place where the Lord rose from the dead. They had been told that Jesus had risen, but they didn't believe it. They were leaving the holy city in desolation (see Lk 24:21), saying, "We thought that he was going to be the one." They had lost their confidence in the Lord Jesus. They had no hope, no faith, no willingness to hear the testimony or to believe in the power of the Resurrection.

The two disciples were so distracted in their disappointment that they couldn't see the mighty works that were already happening in Jerusalem. And they could not recognize Jesus when he began to accompany them. We also get so distracted by our own emotions, disappointments, sorrows, loneliness, and anxiety that we can't even see the mighty works of God happening right in front of us.

We have to allow ourselves the eyes of faith. The two disciples had abandoned belief in the Lord, yet he sought them out. What a powerful display of love! The Lord went to them, searched for them, sought to walk with them. He began a journey with them.

The Lord Jesus seeks us out, too, even in our darkest hours. While we can be unfaithful, he is always faithful to us. He wants to journey with us. He wants to walk with us, to be a part of our lives and make us strong. He seeks to fill us up with immense hope and a zealous sense of mission.

So often, we think that God is supposed to come and make everything easy, comfortable, and luxurious. When it isn't so, we shake our fist at the heavens or are downcast in our souls, saying to ourselves, "How could God allow these things to happen?" We get distracted, yet Jesus says to us: "Oh, you foolish of heart, do you not know that this is a fallen world? This is not the end. This is not heaven. There will be suffering in this life so that there can be redemption." This is the reason for our hope and the source of our peace.

As the two disciples reached Emmaus, they asked the Lord to stay with them, since the night was coming. The Lord who sought them out and taught them was now himself being sought out. The hearts of these two disciples had been converted. They had been given new strength. With their hearts now burning, they said to Jesus, "Stay with us."

As we seek to live in peace, this should be the petition of our hearts: "Lord I'm scared, I don't know where things are going. I don't know what's going to happen in my life or in our world. Lord, it feels as if I've lost everything. The day is far spent and night is falling. Stay with me, Lord. Help me!"

Wisdom for Our Lives

As we walk through life burdened by disappointment, weariness, and loneliness, we can still look for the Lord. No matter how we feel, he is present, and he seeks to accompany us. Let's ask for the grace to recognize this, so that we can live in peace even in our darkest moments.

PRAYER
Heavenly Father,
The journey of life is marked with so many
    struggles.
Help us not to become overwhelmed.
Give us your strength.
Lord Jesus,
you are our Friend and constant Companion.
Help us to recognize your presence.
Convert our hearts.
Set them on fire with your love.
Help us to be strong in you.
Walk with us.
Show us the Father.
Point us to the joys of Paradise.
Save us!
For you are Lord, forever and ever.
Amen.

··IV··

THE CARE OF OUR
GOOD SHEPHERD

But he who enters by the door is the shepherd
of the sheep. To him the gatekeeper opens;
the sheep hear his voice, and he calls his own
sheep by name and leads them out.

John 10:2–3

When I was a child, my siblings and I played out-
side — often until the streetlights came on. We
were a military family, so we traveled to various
duty assignments. On one such assignment, we
lived in an apartment building that overlooked
a huge playground; it was awesome! Every kid
wanted to be there, and, at any one time, there
could be dozens of children whooping and holler-
ing. You can imagine all the noise and yelling and
screaming that happened on that playground.

Yet, with all that noise and chaos, if my mom opened the window from our apartment and yelled our names, we would hear her voice. And certainly, if she walked down to the playground and called us, we would immediately recognize her voice and stop what we were doing. We knew our mother's voice, no matter what was happening. And the same thing happened if it was our father calling us. We knew his voice. If we heard, we knew to stop and, almost involuntarily, run to him.

Children tend to recognize the voice of their parents. It should be a voice associated with love, safety, comfort, encouragement, and care. And just as children hear and respond to the call of their parents, we can use this experience as a way to recognize the voice of the Lord.

In John's Gospel, the Lord announces that he is the Good Shepherd. As the Good Shepherd, he wants his sheep to come to him. He calls them by name, and they know his voice (see 10:3). As members of his fold, we know the Lord's voice as a voice of comfort, consolation, protection, and safety.

The Lord tells us about the robbers and

Sell your books at sellbackyourBook.com!
Go to sellbackyourBook.com
and get an instant price
quote. We even pay the
shipping - see what your old
books are worth today!

00064846017

C-2
S-1

6017

0006484

thieves who try to sneak in to scare or scatter us. But our Good Shepherd, who seeks to unite the fold and form a new community, leads and guides us along safe and good paths. This Good Shepherd is the Risen Christ. And he calls each one of us by name. As members of his community, we hear his voice and recognize it amidst all the noise and darkness of our fallen world.

Through all the insecurities, uncertainties, and fears that surround our hearts, the Good Shepherd calls. When we cry out, "I'm scared. I don't know what's going to happen. When is this going to pass? The walls are beginning to close in," the Lord Jesus breaks through. He calls us back to our senses, back to hope, back to his peace. He calls each of us by name, and we are invited to raise our heads and respond to him, to run to him and seek his love.

But do we hear his voice? For some, the Good Shepherd calls and his voice sounds like so many other voices in our world. When we can't recognize his voice, we think: "Who is that person — who is calling my name? How do they know my name? What do they want?"

Or perhaps the voice sounds faintly familiar. We hear it and think: "Wait a minute, who's calling my name? That voice somehow resonates in my heart. I think I know that voice. It sounds familiar, but I can't quite place it. Who is calling my name?"

For those who do not know the voice of the Good Shepherd, his call is a perpetual opportunity to come to know and encounter him. Now is the time to hear his voice, to see his eyes looking upon you, and to enter into a powerful and dynamic relationship with him. For those who recognize the voice, but aren't sure who is calling, now is the time to realize that this is the voice of the Good Shepherd, who calls you, who wants you to be a part of his community, and who wants to keep you safe and protect you and guide you. You are invited to reignite your relationship with him.

Perhaps you have already heard and recognized his voice. Perhaps you want to follow him. He empowers you and calls you to deeper fellowship with him and to the task of continuing his work.

This is not a time for fear, self-pity, or anxiety. We are all the children of God. The Lord has come, and he has destroyed sin and death so that we might live. He offers us an abundance of life. Our task is to dispel the bad spirits in our hearts, and to dive into the grace and love that our Good Shepherd offers to us. We must allow him to work in our souls today.

The Bible also warns us about the robbers and thieves, who sneak into the fold and scare the sheep because they're strangers. As children, we were often told that if a stranger was to approach us and call our names, we were to shout, "Stranger, danger!" We were to tell the person to stop talking to us, and if they kept calling our names, we were to run for help.

If we don't know someone, we don't know their intentions. We don't know what they're going to do to us. This is why strangers provoke fear, especially when they know our names. Regrettably, for many people in our world today, Jesus Christ is that stranger. They are frightened by the Risen Christ, the Good Shepherd who calls out to us, and in their hearts they yell out, "Stranger, danger!"

As believers, we have to be careful that we do

not allow the Risen Christ to become a stranger. We have to hear his voice, recognize him, and allow ourselves to be shepherded by him. And as we allow Christ to shepherd us, we are called to be shepherds ourselves.

The Lord sends us out into the world to be salt, light, and leaven. We must go to those who are scared and declare words of hope and peace. We are sent to those who are alone to be their friend. We are commissioned to go to the person who feels abandoned and accompany them. We must seek out those who have no love and show them a generous love. We are called to be shepherds.

This starts at home. As Christians we are a grassroots people. We love our neighbor — their annoying habits, their bad breath, and everything that goes with them. While our call to shepherd others is a summons to the whole world, it begins with those closest to us. It means husbands shepherd their wives, and wives shepherd their husbands. It means that parents are called to shepherd their children. Grandparents are called to shepherd their extended family with the moral authority that God has given them.

Our work begins with our loved ones, and then it expands to friends, coworkers, and neighbors. We are even called to shepherd our enemies by caring for them and seeking their conversion. This is the radical call of the Risen Christ! He has turned our fallen world upside down. The world says, "That person hurt you; curse them." Christ says, "That person hurt you; forgive them and serve them." This world tells us to seek only ourselves, but the Good Shepherd calls us to selflessly serve others and to always go the extra mile.

The fallen world approaches the Gospel message with suspicion, considering it dangerous. But we know that this is a saving message. The path of the Good Shepherd is the path to happiness, virtue, and holiness. It is the path to love and the path to heaven. It is the only path that promises true peace. We can only live this life by dying to our own fallenness. Only then can we hear the voice of the Good Shepherd, who calls us by name, and generously follow him.

Will we let the Risen One shepherd us? Will we accept the call to selflessly shepherd others?

Will we allow the Resurrection to triumph over self-pity and pride? Will we allow love to dispel fear? We decide.

All the power we need has been given to us. The Risen One can destroy the enemies that hurt us. He calls to us. We just have to listen, recognize his voice, and then follow after him. The choice is ours.

Wisdom for Our Lives

The Lord Jesus has destroyed sin and death. He has dispersed darkness and vanquished fear. He is the Good Shepherd. He desires to share his love and joy with us. He calls us by name. Let's ask for the grace to recognize his voice, accept his love, and generously, selflessly follow him.

Prayer

Heavenly Father,
You opened the gate to eternal life.
You sent us your Son as our Good Shepherd.
Dispel the fear and anxiety in our hearts.
Give us hope.
Lord Jesus,

you call to us by name.
Help us to hear your voice.
Open our hearts to acknowledge you.
Shepherd us.
Help us to shepherd others.
Be with us, Lord.
Guide us along your path of love.
Save us! Shepherd us always!
For you are Lord, forever and ever.
Amen.

·· V ··

MARY AND THE GIFT OF PEACE

Let not your hearts be troubled; believe in God,
believe also in me.

John 14:1

Some time ago, my mother had serious back surgery. My brother, sister, and I discussed how we were going to divvy up all her duties while she was in recovery. Most important to this story, my father has dementia, and my mother is his principal caregiver. We had to make sure that my father was taken care of, get the groceries, go to the pharmacy, check the mail, clean and cook … and the list went on. There were so many tasks. Eventually, we sat down and made a list of all the things that needed to be covered.

And we were amazed. Three adult children could barely cover all the tasks that their mother usually accomplished by herself. I was humbled by how hard my mother works for our family. It's important to acknowledge and cherish the vocation of motherhood. God has blessed so many women with this exalted call. In healthy families and societies, hearts are filled with tremendous gratitude for mothers. They are appreciated and loved, revered and shown proper deference.

Of course, as we think about our earthly mothers, our minds very quickly move to our heavenly mother, Mary of Nazareth. Think about the relationship that Jesus and Mary had with each other. It was a relationship of mother and son, parent and child.

Just imagine that relationship. We hear of the endearment. At one point in Our Lord's ministry, someone yells out to him, to paraphrase, "Blessed are the breasts that fed you!" However, the Lord replies, "Blessed rather are those who hear the word of God and keep it!" (see Lk 11:27–28). Jesus is making sure that the praise for his mother is rightly ordered. She is wonderful and good, not because she happened to give birth to Jesus, but because she heard the word of God and believed. She believed in God, and she believed in her Son and his mission.

Mary also worked for Jesus and his mission. When he ascended to heaven, he left his mother in the Upper Room with his apostles. You can imagine him saying: "Mom, make sure you take care of this Church. Make sure you help them as you helped me. Guide this Church. Help them. They're broken, confused, and scared. Take care of them." And he made sure that his mother received the power of the Holy Spirit with the apostles. She received it for her own vocation as Mother of the Church. And Mary continues to guide us, just as she guided the Lord Jesus throughout his earthly life.

Do you ever think of the difficulty of Our Lady's life? To have a child who is immediately threatened? To have to flee to a foreign land (Egypt), to a language, a people, and culture she didn't know, in order to keep him safe? And then to come home and have to make further adjustments because the threat is still impending? And to continue to raise this child, knowing that he is destined for greatness and for glory, but also for great suffering?

Imagine our Lady at Calvary. Our Church hails her at Calvary as *Stabat Mater* ("Standing Mother"). I don't like the images that show Mary wailing and crestfallen at the cross. I don't think that was her attitude. I think she knew exactly what was going to happen, and the Lord had fashioned and created her heart for that very moment. Certainly, Mary was in sorrow, her Immaculate Heart suffering with the Lord, but she knew who her Son was, and she knew the power that he held over all things, even death. Mary knew that he would rise again.

The Lord promises us peace. He wants to bless us with consolation. He does not want our hearts to be troubled by any of the difficulties of this life. And to help us discover peace, he gives us his mother as an example and guide. Mary stands as the Queen of Peace. Do you think the Immaculate Heart of Our Lady was troubled by the things of this world? No. It was so full of God's grace, so full of peace, that it had no room for darkness, self-pity, bitterness, resentment, or entitlement. Mary had too many good things to do. Her focus was always on the peace that comes from above.

In similar fashion, we also have much to do! Today, with the intercession of Our Lady, let's accept the Lord's invitation to peace. He tells us, "Let not your hearts be troubled." The Lord has conquered the kingdom of sin and death. He has dispelled darkness. And he offers us the gift of peace. This is a peace that allows for a tranquility of order. It's a peace that shows us how much we are loved and that constantly calls us to love those around us.

Let not your hearts be troubled. Accept the gift of peace today. And then fight and let nothing disturb you. Hold on to the gift of peace, as Our Lady did. Even as she saw her Son brutally crucified, she could still be *Stabat Mater*, because in her heart, peace triumphed. So, too, in our suffering and hardship, if we allow it, God's peace will triumph. The hearts of Jesus and Mary will triumph. But we have to accept peace. We have to calm our hearts and realize what is offered to us. And today the Risen Christ, through the intercession of his mother, offers us peace. We are called to graciously, generously, profoundly, and unconditionally accept that peace and let it triumph in our hearts and in our homes.

Wisdom for Our Lives

The Lord Jesus has blessed us with his own mother to help us and guide us in every trial we face in this life. She is our mother and the Queen of Peace. Let's turn to her and ask for her encouragement and intercession as we seek to live the Lord's peace in our lives.

Prayer

Heavenly Father,

You sent us your Son.

Help us to accept your gift of peace in our hearts.

Free us from the anxiety and distress of our
      world.

Give us the help of your grace.

Lord Jesus, you are the Risen One,

who has conquered the world.

You blessed us with your own Mother,

who stood boldly with you in your Passion.
Give us her strength and guidance.
Help us to turn to you and to preserve your
    peace.
Bless us in the sufferings and sorrows of this life.
Mother Mary, Queen of Peace,
pray for us, teach us, encourage us!
Through Christ our Lord.
Amen.

·· VI ··

No Longer Orphans

I will not leave you orphans;
I will come to you.

John 14:18 (NABRE)

We have good news! Our God is a loving Father who is tremendously in love with each of us. He wants to care for us and help us along the path of life, with all its joys and sorrows.

We are not orphans. We live in a fallen world, caused by our own sin, and that means bad things happen. It means that we will have hurricanes, tornadoes, tsunamis, pandemics, cancer, dementia, financial problems, betrayal, divorce, and other heartbreaking difficulties. So many terrible and hard things happen in a fallen world. And at times, if we allow the fallen state of this world to take over our hearts, it can lead us into desolation and even despair, wondering: Is there even a God? Why does he allow this evil to happen? Why doesn't he do something?

We further wonder: How am I supposed to continue with my life? How is this all going to come back together?

The fallenness of this world seeks to overtake us, eclipse our hearts, and drag us into darkness. But we are the children of God! We are not orphans, because God our Father has sent his Son to give us the power of his grace. Grace is God's life within us. It gives us the strength to fight, to persevere, and to be instruments of goodness. And this is our task. As Christian believers, we don't have time to wallow in the darkness of this fallen world. We have been called to the riches of God's glory and to the peace that comes from his grace. We are the children of God.

And so, when this fallen world wants to whisper to our hearts that we are orphans — abandoned, no longer loved — we can tell that fallen spirit to go to hell, where it belongs. Because we are the children of God. We are not orphans. By God's grace, we will conquer. God's light dispels the darkness and gives us hope. This world's difficulties and sorrows will pass, but God's grace remains, and this is the source of our peace.

Do we realize that we have been made for eternity? Do we fully understand that the things of this world are given to us in order to prepare us for eternal life? Do we let ourselves experience the wonder of being a child of our Father in heaven and a sibling to our older brother, Jesus Christ? The Holy Spirit has been sent upon us, and his grace is being poured into our hearts. We have all that we need to allow goodness to triumph over evil, and for peace to vanquish anxiety.

We are called to continue to fan into flame the great hope and immense joy that has been given us by God. We must regularly claim our inheritance as the children of God, and live according to his way of love and peace. We should not live or conduct ourselves as spiritual orphans.

We must stand firm, know who we are, and realize how much we are loved. We are the children of God, and we need to allow his grace to work in our lives for our own salvation, so that we can become instruments of his hope and peace in the world today.

Isn't this exciting? This is our moment! The fallen state of this world has convinced so many people that they're unlovable, that they're abandoned, and that there is no hope. But this is the moment for the Christian message to shine out to all the world. This is especially our moment to once again share the saving message of Jesus Christ, to once again announce to the world that we are the children of God and that this reality is the source of our peace.

WISDOM FOR OUR LIVES

We are the children of God. We hold an identity beyond the tragedies, difficulties, sorrows, and disappointments of this world. The Lord Jesus is our older brother. He saves us from the sin and darkness of the fallen world and shows us the peace, hope, and abiding light of our heavenly Father. Let's turn to the Lord and ask him for the help of his grace as we live out our inheritance as the children of God.

PRAYER

Heavenly Father,

You have called us to yourself.

We are not orphans. We are your children.

You claim us as members of your family,

and you call us to live according to your way of
    love and peace.

Lord Jesus,

you are true Savior and true older brother to us.

You save us from the darkness of our world,

and you show us how to live as the children of
    our Father.

Give us the help of your grace.

Remove anxiety and desolation from our hearts.

Bless us with your peace!

For you are Lord, forever and ever.

Amen.

·· VII ··

Go and Teach

*All authority in heaven and on earth has been
given to me. Go therefore and make disciples
of all nations ... teaching them to observe all
that I have commanded you; and behold, I am
with you always, to the close of the age.*
Matthew 28:18–20

As we watch the fallenness of our world play
itself out in pandemics, racism, violence on our
streets, political tension, distrust and disuni-
ty among neighbors, we can discern a certain
pattern in our own responses. This pattern has
been recognized in our spiritual tradition for
ages. Contemporary therapists have picked up
on it. It has been especially explained by Dr.
Elisabeth Kübler-Ross.

The pattern is fairly straightforward:

There's an initial shock, then denial, anger, depression (more properly called melancholy in our spiritual tradition), bargaining and testing, and finally surrender.

As we witness the darkness, we feel an initial shock: "What is happening? What am I seeing? This can't be real!" Then, denial: "No, this isn't really happening. It's not really that bad. It's okay. There must be some reason or explanation." And then, anger: "Why was this allowed to happen? Why didn't our leaders protect us? Why didn't we see this coming?" Next, there's melancholy: "Life just isn't worth living. I don't even want to get out of bed anymore. I don't understand the point of all this. Will this ever end? Where is God?" And then, there's the bargaining and the testing: "Lord, if you let this pass, I'll be a better Catholic. Lord, if you please hurry this up and just let me have this part, or be there, or see this person, then I'll be a better person. Lord, just give me this one thing and I'll give you whatever you want." And, finally, we move to a state of acceptance: "This is really happening. I surrender. What is my part? What do I need to do?"

We see this pattern play itself out often in our world. We know that there are many who get stuck in certain stages. Some remain in perpetual denial. Others are in a constant state of anger. Still others are frozen in melancholy.

As the children of God, who have received the divine gift of peace, we are called out of darkness and into the light. We are called to accept the bad things of this world, as we recognize that the only power they have over us is the very power we give them.

But what does acceptance look like? Yes, we are living in a fallen world. There are ups and downs and possible regressions. Various people keep waiting for some magic answer, some news flash that will fix everything, or some medical, political, or financial solution that will solve all our problems, as if we can simply flip a switch and everything becomes better. But that's not how life in a fallen world truly works.

There are sorrows and tragedies, unexpected twists and turns, loss and grieving. Life as we know it is constantly changing, and we rarely have any power to stop it, pause it, or fix it. Life is regularly ending, and parts of it die with time. Our task is to allow ourselves to grieve and to allow it to die. It's only when we are willing to accept the reality of this fallen world — the here and now — that we can begin to find the peace that is beyond this world. As we acknowledge the things that change, we can discern and discover the peace that never changes. As we identify the bad news of our world, we are able to see and cherish the good news that is offered to us in Jesus Christ, the Risen One.

As Christians, we are called to accept the shock, hurt, melancholy, and anger in our world and in our hearts. We have to acknowledge our own fear and anxiety. These are real emotions and true states of our soul. We cannot hide or remain in denial. We must admit the anguish, disillusionment, and sorrow in our hearts.

Only then can we honestly turn to God and ask for his healing and strength. Our hearts must be transparent if they are going to be truly open. And we want our hearts to be open, for God is only able to heal open hearts.

Our faith teaches us acceptance in the face

of evil and death. But God has not only taught us how to die. In Jesus Christ, he has taught us how to rise and how to live!

As we welcome God's healing in our hearts, we are given the gift of peace. As Christians, we acknowledge the happenings of our world. We name the things in our heart. We ask God to show us the way. Yes, we are given healing, true surrender, peace, and life, but we are also given a mission. The Lord Jesus tells us to go and teach all nations (see Mt 28:18–20).

As Christians, the sons and daughters of God, and instruments of peace, we don't have the time or interest to wallow in the fallenness of this world. We are called and empowered to conquer the desolation and despair of the world. We are given God's grace, and we are told by the Lord to get about the Father's business. It's time for us to be attentive. We are people on a mission. We live with purpose. We refuse the false peace of self-pity, entitlement, and bitterness.

So, what can we do to live a life of true peace? How can we accept God's healing and share his peace with others? We can start with

small, simple steps: Get up; set a schedule; or-
ganize your prayers; go for a walk; read a book;
study the Scriptures; reach out to the poor; seek
out a neighbor who is alone. We have a great
mission! We don't have time to dialogue with
darkness because we have been made for greater
things.

We have been made for grace. We have
been made for glory. And the Lord Jesus, true
God and true man, blesses us with peace and
shows us our eternal home. The brokenness and
the fallenness and the sinfulness of this world
should make us uncomfortable, because this
is not heaven. This darkness is not our home.
Therefore, we cannot allow the fallen state of
our world eclipse our peace or distract us from
eternity.

We are the children of God, and we have
work to do!

Wherever we have been, whatever darkness
we have allowed in our hearts, now is the time
to let the light and beauty of God's grace enter
our souls and give us a new direction, a divine
peace, an eternal hope. Now is the time to leave

the darkness behind and to enter into God's own marvelous light.

We are the children of God, the sons and daughters of the Resurrection. Heaven awaits us, and the work of God is before us. Let's get to work!

Wisdom for Our Lives

We have been called out of darkness into God's own marvelous light. The sorrows of this world are healed by God's grace. We are blessed with his peace. As we receive such gifts, we are called to share them. We are commissioned; we are sent. Let's ask Jesus for his tenacity and trust in the Father as we continue his mission on earth.

Prayer

Heavenly Father,
You sent us your Son.
You have given us your peace.
You now call us to share in your mission.
Help us to reveal your love to our world.
Lord Jesus, you always did the will of the
  Father.

You ransomed us from darkness.

You are our friend and companion.

You now commission us.

You compel us to give to others what we have
    received.

Help us to be faithful and generous in sharing
    your message.

Bless us with your peace!

For you are Lord, forever and ever.

Amen.

Conclusion

As believers in Jesus Christ, we see and acknowledge the evils of our day and the real consequences they have in our hearts, but we understand that these are the tragic consequences of a fallen world. The grace of God and the promise of eternal glory break through these sorrows.

Darkness seeks to overtake our hearts, but we can repel it with God's grace. We boldly proclaim our identity as sons and daughters of God. We claim the power of the Resurrection and use this power to disperse darkness, overcome desolation, receive the divine gift of peace, and dwell in the hope of heaven.

We were not made for the sorrows of this world. We were made for glory and for eternity. By keeping our focus on heaven, our higher natures, and on the grace of God, we are emboldened to receive and to confidently announce the Good News of Jesus Christ.

Sin and death have been defeated. The fallenness of this world does not have the last word.
We are not orphans in a lost world. We are the
children of God, on a mission in this world to
proclaim peace, salvation, and hope. We are the
children of God on our way to heaven.

I pray the reflections in this small book have
been a help to you, dear reader, in seeking to live
in God's peace. I pray that whatever sorrows
or sufferings you might be enduring now, that
you might always find the peace of God within
you. May that peace, which is beyond all understanding, strengthen you and help you through
the evils of our day. By conquering them in the
Lord's peace, may you become a more credible
and energetic witness to the saving message of
Jesus Christ!

ABOUT THE AUTHOR

Fr. Jeffrey Kirby, STD, is a Papal Missionary of Mercy, pastor of Our Lady of Grace Parish in Indian Land, South Carolina, and a senior contributor to the *Crux* news site. He is the author of several books, including *Kingdom of Happiness: Living the Beatitudes in Everyday Life.*